10-01
12/01

HIST

9/03
1

CELEBRITY BIOS

Keri Russell

Judy Parker

HIGH
interest
books

Children's Press
A Division of Scholastic Inc.
New York / Toronto / London / Auckland / Sydney
Mexico City / New Delhi / Hong Kong
Danbury, Connecticut

To Claire, who made it happen

Book Design: Michael DeLisio
Contributing Editor: Matthew Pitt

Photo Credits: Cover © Reuters NewMedia Inc./Corbis; pp. 4, 37 © Steve Granitz/Retna Ltd; pp. 8-9, 10, 11, 14, 16, 19, 20, 23, 31, 34 © The Everett Collection; p. 13 © Janet Macoska/Retna Ltd.; p. 24 © AFP/Corbis; p. 26 © AP/Wide World Photos; p. 29 © John Marshall Mantel/Corbis; p. 32 © Bill Davila/Retna Ltd.; p. 39 © John Spellman/Retna Ltd.

Visit Children's Press on the Internet at:
http://publishing.grolier.com

Library of Congress Cataloging-in-Publication Data

Parker, Judy.
  Keri Russell / Judy Parker.
    p. cm. -- (Celebrity bios)
  Includes index.
  ISBN 0-516-23428-5 (lib. bdg.) -- ISBN 0-516-29603-5 (pbk.)
  1. Russell, Keri, 1976---Juvenile literature. 2. Actors--United
States--Biography--Juvenile literature. [1. Russell, Keri, 1976–2. Actors and
  actresses. 3. Women-- Biography.] I. Title. II. Series.

  PN2287.R825 P37 2001
  791.45'028'092--dc21
  [B]
                                                    2001017486

CONTENTS

CHAPTER ONE

A Talented Woman

"I think in movement. I always have music on. Even when I'm getting ready to shoot a scene, I'll listen to certain music to get ready."
—Keri in the Seattle Times

Keri Russell is a very talented young woman. She has packed a lot of success into the first twenty-five years of her life. Keri is best known as the star of the television show "Felicity." She is also an accomplished, or well-trained, dancer and photographer.

Here, Keri shows off her glamorous side. She attends the Emmy Awards in a dazzling floor-length dress.

A LOVE OF DANCE

Keri Russell was born in Fountain Valley, California, on March 23, 1976. Her father, David, had a job that sometimes forced the family to move. Keri's family lived in Texas when she was little, but eventually they moved to Mesa, Arizona. David and Stephanie, Keri's mother, raised Keri, her brother, Todd, and her sister, Julie.

In Mesa, Keri enjoyed athletics such as softball and track. She also began to study jazz dance and ballet. Dance helped Keri to find new ways of expressing herself. It also boosted her self-esteem. Keri told *In Style* that she thought it was "hugely important for a teenage girl to have something more important in her life than junior high." Keri's skills landed her a spot on the Mesa Stars Dance and Drill Team. She performed at football games and other school events.

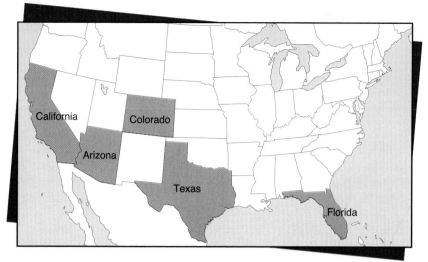

Keri has lived and worked in states from coast to coast.

WORKING FOR DISNEY

When Keri was fifteen, her father's company asked him to move to Colorado. The Russells moved to a town near Denver. The transition, or change, was hard for Keri. She attended Highlands Ranch High School but didn't feel that she fit in. "All through high school, I felt very alienated," she revealed to *Teen People*. She continued dancing but looked for other ways to be creative.

A fashion photographer who noticed Keri suggested that she should try modeling. This led to some tryouts, or auditions. However,

Keri wasn't happy modeling. She found an agent who arranged other auditions for her. Keri soon got a part on the Disney Channel's "The All New Mickey Mouse Club" series.

"The All New Mickey Mouse Club" was taped in Orlando, Florida. Performing on the show was a demanding job. Keri had to spend half of each year in Orlando, away from her family and friends. Yet the show gave Keri a chance to use her dancing skills and perform with talented co-stars. Some of those co-stars

included Justin Timberlake and J.C. Chasez—future members of the singing group 'N Sync. Keri also worked with Christina Aguilera and Britney Spears before they shot to stardom.

Tony Lucca was another one of Keri's co-stars. While performing together, Tony and Keri fell in love. "We kissed when we were both fifteen," she told *In Style*. They didn't date very seriously while they were on the Disney show. Yet it was the beginning of a very important relationship in Keri's life.

Keri (fourth from the right) got her first taste of performing as a cast member of "The All New Mickey Mouse Club."

Keri made her motion picture debut in *Honey, I Blew Up the Kid.*

L.A. WOMAN

While working on "Mickey Mouse Club," Keri was cast in her first movie. It was Disney's *Honey, I Blew Up the Kid.* The movie was successful, and Keri was considered for other major roles. In 1993, when she was seventeen, Keri left "Mickey Mouse Club" and moved to Los Angeles. She knew that Los Angeles was the best place for an actress to find work. She immediately began to audition. Keri got a part as a guest star on the popular TV show "Boy Meets World." She also got a role on a new TV show called "Emerald Cove."

A Talented Woman

Though "Emerald Cove" didn't last long, Keri bounced back. She was soon cast in another new TV series, "Daddy's Girls." Her co-star was the famous British actor Dudley Moore. Keri played the part of one of Dudley's daughters. The reviewers liked Keri, but the series didn't do well in the ratings. Because of this, it was canceled, or taken off the air. Keri had to look for work again!

In 1995, Keri was cast in the television movie *The Babysitter's Seduction*. In the movie, she falls in love with the father of the kids she baby-sits. Keri again worked with famous actors,

Keri gives her TV dad Dudley Moore a bear hug.

including Stephen Collins ("7th Heaven"). Collins had worked with hundreds of actresses.

However, when he saw Keri, he knew she had star quality. Following *The Babysitter's Seduction*, Keri got great news! She was cast in the lead role of an Aaron Spelling TV series, "Malibu Shores."

BIG BREAK OR BIG BREAKUP?

Aaron Spelling is a producer who has created some of the most successful TV series ever. His hits include "Charlie's Angels," "Beverly Hills 90210," "7th Heaven," and "Charmed." Keri was cast as Chloe Walker on "Malibu Shores." Chloe was a rich girl who fell in love with a middle-class boy from the suburbs. There were high hopes for "Malibu Shores." Keri kept her fingers crossed. Unfortunately, the show wasn't a hit. It was canceled after just ten episodes.

The series wasn't the only thing that came to an end. Keri had been living with Tony Lucca in Los Angeles. Tony was one of Keri's "Malibu

Many people in Hollywood were surprised that "Malibu Shores" was not a hit. Here, Keri (center) poses with her co-stars.

Shores" co-stars. They again were working side by side. However, the pressures of living and working together were too much for the couple. They ended their relationship. "We didn't talk for quite a while," Keri said in an interview for *In Style*.

Keri was feeling some acting pressures, too. She was working, but she couldn't find a successful TV series after leaving "Mickey Mouse Club." She didn't give up, though. In 1996, she was cast in the TV movie version of the famous Shirley Jackson story "The Lottery." Keri's co-star was Dan Cortese of the TV shows

In 1996, Keri and Dan Cortese were co-stars in the
TV movie *The Lottery*.

"Melrose Place" and "Veronica's Closet." In 1997, Keri appeared on the pilot episode of the Fox TV series "Roar." However, this job didn't last very long. Her character was killed in the first episode!

MORE MOVIES

In 1997, Keri also made a movie called *Eight Days a Week*. It was about a teenage boy who becomes obsessed with his beautiful neighbor (played by Keri). *Eight Days a Week* wasn't released for more than a year after the actors were finished. Keri received good reviews when audiences finally saw the movie.

Keri soon got another movie role. In *Mad About Mambo*, Keri played an Irish dancer who enters a Latin dance competition. After her dance partner is injured, she gets a new partner. The new partner is a soccer player who is learning dance to improve his athletic ability.

Keri got to dance up a storm in *Mad About Mambo*.

Keri's character falls in love with him. The part gave Keri a chance to combine her dancing and acting skills. She also had to learn an Irish accent for the part. As with *Eight Days a Week*, *Mad About Mambo* wasn't released until after Keri started working on "Felicity." Many reviewers thought that Keri's performance was the best part of the movie.

CHANCE OF A LIFETIME

In 1998, Keri had the chance to audition for a new series on The WB network. The WB had produced two very successful series for teenagers—"Buffy the Vampire Slayer" and "Dawson's Creek." The new series was created for a slightly older audience. It was about a young woman's first year of college. The series was named after the main character, Felicity.

Keri's character, Felicity, is intelligent but impulsive. In the pilot, Felicity suddenly decides to give up her plans of going to medical school. Instead, she follows her high school crush across the country to New York City.

The producers had a hard time finding an actress who could portray all of Felicity's different qualities. They auditioned hundreds of women. J.J. Abrams, a co-creator of "Felicity," spoke with *Teen People* about Keri's audition. He said that Keri was "vulnerable and confused—but also strong. She just owned the part."

The producers were impressed with Keri. However, they were concerned that she was too beautiful to play Felicity. Yet no other actress was able to perform the part the way Keri could. The producers called her back to read the lines again and again. Keri was excited but nervous. Finally, she got a message from her agent—she had the part!

Keri was excited to have a leading role. However, she knew how show business worked. Many new television series are canceled quickly. She knew this from personal experience. Little did she know what big changes were about to happen. At the age of twenty-two, Keri Russell was about to become TV's newest star!

Did you know?

Keri has a music video credit, too. In 1994, she appeared in the hit video for the Bon Jovi song "Always." At one point, groceries are tossed at her!

In 1998, The WB network gave Keri her biggest acting break. They cast her as the title character of the show "Felicity."

CHAPTER TWO

Sudden Stardom

"Felicity is making that huge choice to be independent and grow. No matter what age or what type of person you are, anyone can relate to that." —*Keri in* **Teen People**

KERI AND THE CAST

Keri wasn't the only one to audition several times for her role on "Felicity." Scott Foley—who plays Felicity's dorm advisor, Noel—was considered for more than one part. Foley originally auditioned for Ben, the high school crush who is followed by Felicity to New York. In the

"Felicity" is set on an imaginary college campus called The University of New York.

end, the part of Ben went to Scott Speedman, a Canadian actor. The part of Felicity's best friend, Julie, went to actress Amy Jo Johnson. Tangi Miller was cast as the grumpy New Yorker, Elena.

GETTING NOTICED

The cast had good chemistry from the start. "We hang out [together]," Keri told *Teen People*. "Amy Jo plays guitar and sings at some local places and we all go check it out." The producers were very happy with the pilot episode of "Felicity." The critics and TV station owners were also happy with the pilot. They gave it great reviews.

Even before the show began, fans started noticing Keri. People approached her on the street after reading articles about her. They asked for her autograph. Keri enjoyed the new attention, but sometimes it felt too intense.

Critics were instantly impressed with Keri's work on "Felicity."

The first episode of "Felicity" aired in September 1998, following "Buffy the Vampire Slayer." The ratings were not as high as the producers hoped, but many critics had good things to say. Most critics felt that the show was smart and funny. Nearly all of them thought that Keri was perfect for the part. A *Time* magazine critic even said that Keri was "a fine actor [with a] touch of bliss that falls from the heavens."

Those critics turned out to be right. Only three months after the show began, "Felicity" and Keri both were nominated for Golden

Keri was walking on air after she won a Golden Globe Award in 1999.

Globe Awards. In January, Keri won the Golden Globe Award for Best Actress in a Drama Series. She was completely surprised. "I need to sit down. I'm in shock," she told an *In Style* reporter after winning.

Keri had acted on TV for many years. She was prepared for the long hours it took to tape "Felicity." Sometimes she worked for fifteen hours a day. Though she was a celebrity, Keri didn't go to many late-night parties. After such a long workday, Keri was ready to go to sleep!

A ROLE MODEL

Keri hoped that her character would be a positive influence on young women. When she first got the part, she helped the costumers decide what Felicity should look like. Keri was upset that many women's magazines featured only models who were extremely thin. She told *Jump* magazine that she wanted Felicity to be more like real young women. "I love the fact that my character

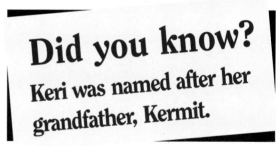

Did you know?
Keri was named after her grandfather, Kermit.

doesn't wear makeup. I love that she puts her hair back, that she wears big baggy sweaters and tennis shoes."

The style created for Felicity's character is a lot like Keri's personal style. Keri very rarely wears makeup. "Makeup doesn't feel pretty to me," she says. "Women look so much better as

The "Felicity" cast is a close-knit group.

they are." She is much happier in jeans and sweaters than in expensive dresses. She enjoys spending time outdoors, hiking, and playing sports. She uses all of these things to add a touch of reality to her character.

CHANGE OF HEART

During the show's first season, Felicity was torn between two men. There was Ben, the high school crush she'd followed to New York, and Noel, her dorm's resident advisor. Keri's own romantic life seemed to be much simpler. She and Tony Lucca were back together. Tony was pursuing a career as a singer-songwriter. Keri and Tony often were seen together. They both wore silver friendship rings. Keri thought of Tony as her best friend.

However, Keri and Tony quietly broke up again. Keri would not give details about her private life. After Tony moved out of the house they shared, Keri focused on herself. "It's time to grow as an individual. I don't want to be married right now," she said. Keri enjoyed her time alone as well as the company of close friends.

Keri's romantic life picked up in the fall of 2000. There was a new man in Keri's life—her

"Felicity" co-star, Scott Speedman! At the end of the show's second season, Felicity and Ben got together. Both stars were quiet about the relationship. Though it recently ended, Scott and Keri remained good friends.

DEALING WITH HYPE

During the first year of "Felicity," Keri took a crash course in being famous. She had to deal with being approached by strangers. Reporters from magazines and newspapers asked her about every detail of her life. Sometimes the tabloids made up stories out of thin air. Keri was polite when she told others to mind their own business. Yet it wasn't always easy.

Keri's popularity exploded. Her face was in magazines everywhere. She was called incredibly beautiful, stylish, and intelligent. It was nice getting this praise. However, it was hard having her private life used to promote a

Keri is generous with her time. Here, she takes a moment
to sign autographs for a few happy fans.

TV show. After she won the Golden Globe
Award, Keri's publicity went through the
roof. "Everyone wants to know, 'How do you
feel about all the hype?'" Keri confessed
to *Entertainment Weekly*. "The truth is,
I don't know."

The hype, or media attention, did have some advantages. At restaurants, Keri didn't have to wait in line. She was always seated right away. She was able to get front-row seats to the best concerts. The royal treatment was exciting, but Keri felt uncomfortable with some of it. Strangers constantly stared at her. At some concerts, the audience watched her more than the band. These things bothered Keri.

HAIR TODAY, GONE TOMORROW

As the second season of "Felicity" began, Keri still had to deal with a lot of hype. One part of Keri got special attention—her beautiful hair.

The beauty magazines focused on her curly locks. There were entire articles about which hair care products Keri used. People wanted to know how she dried her hair after she took a shower.

Keri's most popular feature was about to get even more press. At the start of the second sea-

One of Keri's most famous features was her long hair.

son of "Felicity," Keri cut her famous hair. It wasn't just a trim. Keri chopped it off. She got a super-short cut that was completely different from anything she'd tried before. Keri was reacting to stress by making a big change.

At about the same time, the ratings began to drop. Every week, fewer people tuned in to watch. Perhaps there were many reasons why

the ratings fell. Yet the most important reason was that The WB had moved "Felicity" to Sunday night. On this new night, the show faced tough competition. However, The WB blamed the ratings drop on Keri's haircut. A WB executive said, "You don't want to alter the look of a character from one season to the next. [Felicity's appeal] is enhanced with the longer hair."

The media went wild. Keri sat through dozens of interviews where she was asked only about her hair. She stood by her decision and handled the situation well. "This show is not about a girl who is perfect and pretty," Keri explained to *Teen People*. "It's about a girl who is vulnerable and making mistakes." Keri had no regrets about the haircut. "I did feel exposed ... but I felt much more aware of everything. I'm so glad I did it. No matter what anybody says."

Many people were shocked when Keri got her locks chopped.

CHAPTER THREE

More Than a Star

"The whole point of life is to experience a little bit of everything." —*Keri in* Jump *magazine*

NO MORE SHOW?

After its second season, The WB threatened to cancel "Felicity." The fan response was amazing. Viewers from across the nation flooded the network with phone calls, e-mails, and homemade "Sally tapes." "Sally tapes" are messages recorded on cassettes. They are what Felicity calls the letters she records to her own friend, Sally.

When The WB thought about canceling "Felicity," the show's fans came to the rescue!

The fans had spoken. They convinced The WB to continue airing "Felicity" for a third season. "Felicity" may never be the highest-rated TV show. Yet it will always be number one to its dedicated fans.

SPANNING THE GLOBE

The summer before the third season, Keri traveled a lot. "The weird thing about shooting a series is that you have the summer off," she told *TV Guide Online*. While traveling, Keri pursued another interest of hers—photography. "I really want to travel around the world and take interesting pictures," she revealed to *Jump*.

Did you know?
Keri has starred in several major TV commercials. Some of the spots include ads for Sears, Jack-in-the-Box, and Lee Jeans.

During her summers off from the show, Keri loves to travel.

Keri knows that "Felicity" won't always be on television. She also knows that there are many things she wants to do in life. She wants to continue to make movies and has a couple of projects in the works. One of these projects is a film starring Mel Gibson. The working title for this film is *We Were Soldiers Once...and Young*. It is due for release in December 2001.

Keri has several talents: acting, dancing, and photography. Who knows what Keri will do when the show ends? She may take some time to travel. She may follow in her TV character's footsteps and go to college. Whatever she does, Keri will make her choices with confidence.

Keri Russell plans to stay true to herself. She's confident that her gifts and experience will take her far into the future. "It's not the end-all for me if this [success] falls apart tomorrow," she told *In Style*. With her positive attitude, Keri certainly will have continued success, no matter what she decides to do!

Did you know?

Just like Keri Russell, "Felicity" has gone global! Her television show now airs thousands of miles away in Germany.

Keri has a healthy attitude about her stardom. She knows that even if it ends, she will land on her feet.

1976 • Keri Russell is born on March 23, in Fountain Valley, California.

1991 • Keri moves with her family to Highlands Ranch, a suburb of Denver, Colorado.
• Keri makes her television series debut on "The All New Mickey Mouse Club."

1992 • Keri is cast in the Disney movie *Honey, I Blew Up the Kid.*

1993 • Keri moves to Los Angeles.
• Keri appears on the TV series "Emerald Cove."

1994 • Keri is cast in the TV series "Daddy's Girls."
• Keri is featured in the MTV video for "Always," performed by Bon Jovi.

1995 • Keri makes the TV movie *The Babysitter's Seduction.*

TIMELINE

1996
- Keri co-stars in the TV show "Malibu Shores."

1997
- Keri appears in the movie *Eight Days a Week*.

1998
- In September, "Felicity" debuts on The WB.

1999
- Keri wins the Golden Globe Award for Best Actress in a Drama Series for "Felicity."
- During an episode of the show, Felicity cuts her hair short.
- Keri plays the princess in the children's TV movie *CinderElmo*.

2000
- Keri's film *Mad About Mambo* opens in theaters.
- In the fall, the third season of "Felicity" begins.

FACT SHEET

Name	Keri Lynn Russell
Nickname	Care Bear
Born	March 23, 1976
Birthplace	Fountain Valley, California
Family	Mother, Stephanie; Father, David; Older brother, Todd; Younger sister, Julie
Sign	Aries
Height	5'4"
Hair	Brunette (sometimes blonde)
Eyes	Green

Favorites

Actors	Ethan Hawke
Singers	Tori Amos, Sarah McLachlan, Vince Gill, Bryan Adams
Sports	Basketball and baseball
Foods	Pasta, strawberries
Hobbies	Going to the beach, family barbecues
Pets	Nala, her cat

NEW WORDS

accomplished good at something

agent someone who helps a performer find work

alienated feeling different or left out

auditions tryouts

canceled a show taken off the air

Golden Globe award given by the Hollywood Foreign Press Association

hype attention from the media

pilot the first episode of a new TV series

producer person who creates and supervises movies and television shows

ratings the measure of how many viewers watched a particular show

studio place where a TV show or movie is filmed

tabloids newspapers that rely on gossip instead of fact

transition a major change

FOR FURTHER READING

Furman, Leah. *Meet the Stars of Felicity.* New York: St. Martin's Press, 1999.

Hasday, Judy L. *Keri Russell.* Bear, DE: Mitchell Lane Publishers, 2000.

Krulik, Nancy E. *Scott and Scott: The Boys of* Felicity. New York: Pocket Books, 2000.

Porter, Felicity (Fiction). *Felicity: Summer.* New York: Disney Press, 1999.

Sparks, Kristin. *Felicity and Friends: An Inside Look at TV's Hottest New Show!* New York: Berkley Publishing Group, 1999.

RESOURCES

Web Sites

The Official Web Site of "Felicity"
www.felicity.com
A Web site that keeps you up to date with episodes, message boards, image galleries, and cast bios.

The Keri Russell Home Page
www.kerirussell.net
An easy-to-use Web site that's dedicated to everything about Keri!

RESOURCES

You can also write to Keri at the following address:

Keri Russell
c/o "Felicity"
c/o The WB Television Network
4000 Warner Blvd.
Burbank, CA 91522

INDEX

INDEX

About the Author

Judy Parker has written on a variety of subjects for young adults. She is a Latin music fan and loves to dance salsa.